Diwali

by Rebecca Pettiford

Bullfrog Books

Ideas for Parents and Teachers

Bullfrog Books let children practice reading informational text at the earliest reading levels. Repetition, familiar words, and photo labels support early readers.

Before Reading

- Discuss the cover photo. What does it tell them?

- Look at the picture glossary together. Read and discuss the words.

Read the Book

- "Walk" through the book and look at the photos. Let the child ask questions. Point out the photo labels.

- Read the book to the child, or have him or her read independently.

After Reading

- Prompt the child to think more. Ask: Does your family celebrate Diwali? What sorts of things do you see when people celebrate Diwali?

Bullfrog Books are published by Jump!
5357 Penn Avenue South
Minneapolis, MN 55419
www.jumplibrary.com

Library of Congress Cataloging-in-Publication Data
Pettiford, Rebecca.
  Diwali / by Rebecca Pettiford.
    pages cm.—(Holidays)
  Includes bibliographical references and index.
  Summary: "This photo-illustrated book for early readers describes the Hindu holiday of Diwali and the things people do to celebrate it." Provided by publisher.
  Audience: Age 5-8.
  Audience: Grade K-3.
  ISBN 978-1-62031-132-5 (hardcover)
  ISBN 978-1-62496-197-7 (ebook)
  1. Divali—Juvenile literature. I. Title.
  BL1239.82.D58P48 2015
  394.265'45—dc23
                                        2013049299

Editor: Wendy Dieker
Series Designer: Ellen Huber
Book Designer: Lindaanne Donohoe
Photo Researcher: Kurtis Kinneman

Photo Credits: Tim Gainey/Alamy, 23tl; Ashwin/Shutterstock, 18, 22br; D.Shashikant/Shutterstock, 15, 22tr, 22bl; Hemant Mehta /India Picture/Corbis, 6–7, 14–15; India Picture/Corbis, 8; iStock, 1; Ken Seet/Corbis, 4, 16, 12–13; Malgorzata Kistryn/Shutterstock, 22tl; Nattika/Shutterstock, 17; PaulCowan/iStock, 3; Photosindia.com/SuperStock, 20–21; Shahril KHMD/Shutterstock, 12, 23tr; Shutterstock, cover; Smit/Shutterstock, 23br; Szefei/Shutterstock, 23bl; TheFinalMiracle/Shutterstock, 24; Tim Gainey/Alamy, 10–11, 18–19; Vadim Petrakov, 9; Wong Yu Liang/Shutterstock, 5

Printed in the United States of America at Corporate Graphics in North Mankato, Minnesota.
3-2014
10 9 8 7 6 5 4 3 2 1

Table of Contents

What Is Diwali?

Diwali is a Hindu festival.

It begins in fall.

It lasts five days.

We get ready.

Mom cleans
the house.

She buys
fresh flowers.

Now we can welcome Lakshmi.

Who is Lakshmi?

She is the Hindu goddess of wealth.

She brings good luck.

We light a diya.

A diya is an oil lamp.

The bright lights help Lakshmi find us.

diya

Ali and Roy sit on the floor.

What are they making?

A rangoli. It is art.

rangoli

We shop.

We buy new clothes.

We buy gifts.

Geena eats laddu.

It is sweet like cake. Yum!

laddu

Maya has a sparkler.
Look! Fireworks!

20

Happy Diwali!

Symbols of Diwali

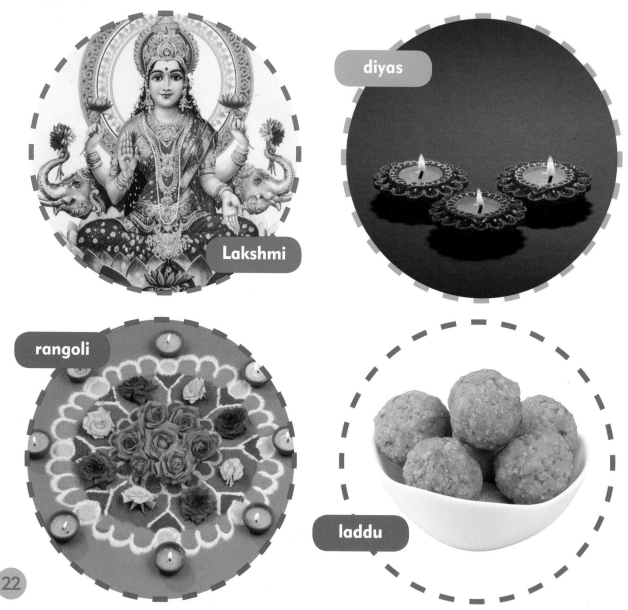

Lakshmi

diyas

rangoli

laddu

Picture Glossary

goddess
A female god.

oil lamp
A light that works by burning oil with a flame, like a candle.

Hindu
A person who follows the Hindu religion. Hindus believe in many gods.

wealth
A large amount of money or possessions.

Index

To Learn More

Learning more is as easy as 1, 2, 3.

1) Go to www.factsurfer.com

2) Enter "Diwali" into the search box.

3) Click the "Surf" button to see a list of websites.

With factsurfer.com, finding more information is just a click away.